The STONE AGE to the BRONZE AGE

The Lives of Ancient People

D0507985

by Ruth Owen

Consultant: James Dilley
University of Southampton
Centre for the Archaeology of Human Origins
www.ancientcraft.co.uk

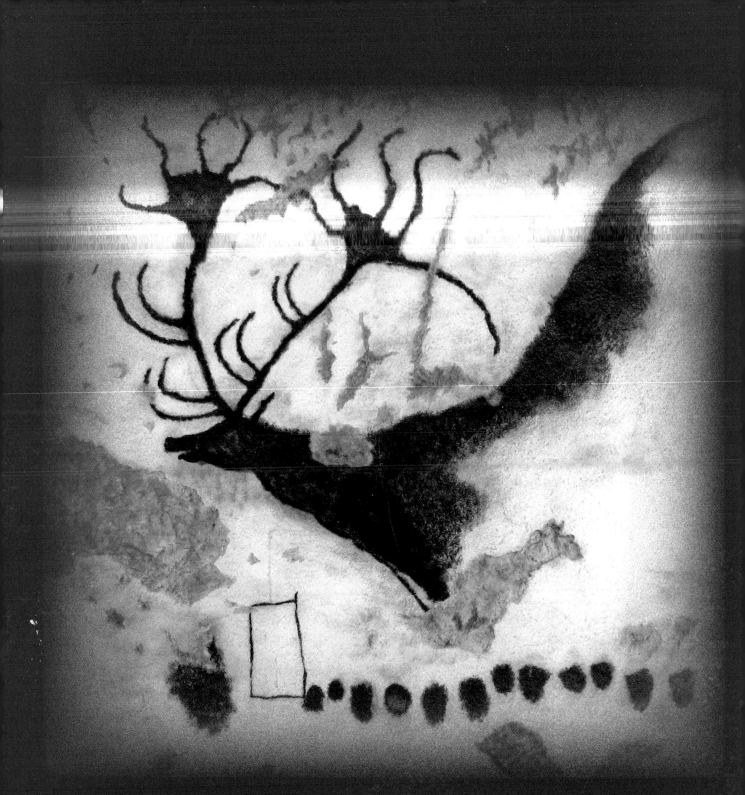

▲ Stone Age art in the Lascaux caves in France

Contents

The Story Begins

In the places where there are now cities, towns, traffic-filled roads and farms, early humans once hunted mammoths, woolly rhinoceroses, reindeer and horses. Welcome to the Stone Age!

Tools Made of Stone

The Stone Age gets its name from the stone tools and weapons made by early humans. Around the world, this period in **prehistory** lasted for more than 3 million years. **Archaeologists** divide the Stone Age into three time periods — the **Palaeolithic**, the **Mesolithic** and the **Neolithic**.

The First Humans in Britain

In the Palaeolithic, Britain was joined to Europe by a wide bridge of land. The first humans came from Europe to Britain across the land bridge about 800,000 years ago.

Groups of early human hunters possibly caught large animals, such as mammoths, by driving them into marshy ground or dead-ends where they became trapped. Then the animals could be killed with spears and other weapons made from wood and stone. Early humans also scavenged on the bodies of large animals that were already dead.

Modern Humans

During the Palaeolithic several different **species** of early humans lived in Britain. Then, about 40,000 years ago the first modern humans (*Homo sapiens*) came from Europe to make Britain their home.

A reconstruction of a woman (*Homo sapiens*) from 40,000 years ago.

Neanderthal Humans

Neanderthals (*Homo neanderthalensis*) were one type of early human that lived in Britain and Europe. Chunky and powerful, Neanderthals were intelligent, knew how to make fire and were skilful toolmakers. They hunted for meat and ate shellfish, plants and fungi. Neanderthals went **extinct** about 40,000 years ago.

Brow ridge sticks out

Big, wide nose

A reconstruction of a Neanderthal man

Early humans wore animal ▶ fur and skins. They made jewellery from shells, antlers, bones and teeth.

Periods of the Stone Age in Britain

The dates of the periods of the Stone Age vary around the world because different **cultures** developed and changed at different speeds. In Britain, most archaeologists use the dates below.

Palaeolithic	Mesolithic	Neolithic
900,000 to 11,500 years ago	11,500 to 6500 years ago	6500 to 4000 years ago

Life in the Palaeolithic

Palaeolithic humans were hunter-gatherers. They hunted for meat and gathered wild berries, nuts, seeds and fungi to eat.

Hunter-Gatherers

Hunter-gatherers moved from place to place to find food. Sometimes they made their homes in caves.

Human Migrations

During the Palaeolithic, the **climate** changed many times — from warm, humid spells to dry, freezing **ice ages**. When survival in one area became too difficult because of lack of food or extreme cold, early humans migrated to a new region.

Stone Age Art

Palaeolithic humans created beautiful paintings on the walls of caves. At the Lascaux caves in France there are nearly 2000 images of humans, animals and mysterious signs, or patterns. The paintings are more than 20,000 years old. The ancient artists probably painted with their fingers, sticks or clumps of moss or hair dipped in paint. They also sprayed paint onto the rock by blowing (or spitting) it from their mouths.

aint was made by mixing water with crushed rocks or soil that contained colourful **pigments**. White clay and black charcoal from fires were also used.

The dark caves were possibly lit by flaming torches or lamps that burned animal fat.

This painting from the Lascaux caves shows an auroch. These large wild cattle are now extinct.

▼

Chunk of flint

Making Tools

Early humans made some of their tools from stone such as flint which could be flaked. They carefully chipped away to shape the flint using another stone (a hammerstone) or a piece of deer antler.

Flaked flint hand axe

An Ice Age in Britain

About 22,000 years ago, Europe was in the grip of the last ice age. Ireland, Wales, Scotland and northern England were covered with a one-kilometre-thick sheet of ice. During this time early humans would have migrated away from Britain to find warmer places to live.

Life in Mesolithic Britain

The Mesolithic period began about 11,500 years ago. At this time, Britain and mainland Europe were connected by Doggerland, an area of land covered with forests and swamps.

Mesolithic Doggerland

Hunter-gatherers lived on Doggerland and used the land bridge to migrate back and forth between Britain and Europe.

Doggerland Disappears

As the last ice age came to an end, temperatures warmed up and the ice sheets covering the land melted, causing sea levels to rise. Gradually, Doggerland became flooded until, about 8500 years ago, Britain and Europe were separated by sea.

As the weather warmed up, forests of pine, birch and alder trees grew across ...tain and parts of Europe.

Map of Doggerland

| | Above sea level 10,000 years ago |
| | Above sea level 9000 years ago |

This map shows Doggerland at the beginning of the Mesolithic period.

Mesolithic people lived in small groups. When they found a place with plenty of food, they made camp.

▲ Mesolithic huts had frames of wooden poles covered with reeds, grasses, bark or animal skins.

Food in the Mesolithic

The mammoths, woolly rhinos and other large prehistoric animals had died out. Now people hunted deer, wild boars and birds, such as ducks and wood pigeons. They fished for salmon and trout in rivers.

Wood pigeon

Wild boar

New weapons were developed for catching fish and small, fast pigs and deer. Tiny, razor-sharp pieces of flint called microliths were glued to wooden shafts with tree resin to make harpoons, spears and arrows.

A reconstruction of a Mesolithic harpoon

Crab apples

Hazelnuts

Women and children foraged for birds' eggs, nuts, berries, crab apples and insects. People who lived on the coast collected shellfish such as limpets.

Dogs in the Stone Age

Scientists believe that wild dogs began living alongside humans about 15,000 years ago. Maybe some brave wolves chose to live near human camps to scavenge food. Perhaps people took wolf cubs from the wild and tamed them. By the Mesolithic period, people hunted with dogs and kept them as pets.

A gray wolf cub

Science Uncovers the Story

The people of the Stone Age left behind no written records. So how do we know how long ago they lived? One way is to use carbon dating.

What Is Carbon Dating?

Carbon dating is a way of working out the age of things that were once living, such as bones or wood. Every living thing contains substances called carbon-12 and carbon-14. When a living thing dies, the carbon-14 starts to decay at a steady, predictable speed. The carbon-12 stays the same. By calculating how much carbon-14 has decayed, scientists can figure out how long a person, animal or plant has been dead.

A 15,000-year-old human skull

A Mesolithic harpoon carved from a reindeer antler

Carbon Dating In Action

Carbon-14 decays by half every 5730 years. Let's say scientists are testing a carved reindeer antler. By comparing the antler's carbon-12 and carbon-14 they can figure out how much carbon-14 was in the antler when the reindeer died. If half that amount still exists, the reindeer has been dead for 5730 years. If a quarter of that amount still exists, the reindeer has been dead for 11,460 years. This means the antler is from the Mesolithic period.

Making Faces with DNA

Scientists can extract **DNA** from an ancient skeleton's bones and teeth. By analysing the DNA **evidence** they can discover details such as a person's hair and eye colour.

Cheddar Man is a skeleton that was found in a cave in Cheddar Gorge in Somerset. Carbon dating showed that he lived in Britain about 10,000 years ago, which means he was a Mesolithic hunter-gatherer. Scientists took DNA from Cheddar Man and discovered that he probably had dark brown hair, dark skin and blue eyes.

Scientists used the DNA evidence and 3D images of Cheddar Man's skull to make this model of his head. ▲

Stone Age Dustbins

Archaeologists sometimes dig up ancient rubbish dumps called **middens**. They find broken tools, animal bones, seashells and even the remains of plants. Just like going through the leftovers in your family's dustbin, archaeologists can tell from the rubbish what ancient people ate. Sometimes they even find **fossilised** human faeces (or poo) that contain seeds, small bones and other clues as to what was on the menu!

The First Farmers

About 12,000 years ago, a momentous change in how humans lived took place. Farming was discovered!

The First Farmers

The idea of settling in one place and producing your own food came from people in Turkey. In time, this knowledge spread around the world.

Archaeologists think that migrants who knew how to farm came to Britain from Europe by boat about 6000 years ago. They brought wheat seeds with them and **domesticated** sheep, goats and cattle.

A New Way of Life

The hunter-gatherer people of Britain became farmers. They caught the wild pigs that roamed Britain's forests and bred them to become domesticated farm animals. In many places, they cut down the forests to clear land for grazing animals and growing crops.

The first sheep in Britain probably looked like this soay sheep.

Archaeologists call this final part of the Stone Age the Neolithic period.

Flint scrapers were used ▶ to scrape meat from animal skins so the skins could be made into leather.

Tools for Farming

Neolithic people developed new stone tools and tool-making techniques to suit their new way of life.

- Chunks of flint and other stones were shaped into axe heads and polished by grinding them against blocks of sandstone. This gave the axe heads sharper edges for cutting down trees.

- The ground was tilled (broken up) with wooden ploughs and seeds were sown by hand.

Wooden handle

Polished axe head

Sharp flint blades are set into the sickle's wooden handle.

- Crops were harvested with curved sickles.

Wheat

- Wheat was threshed using sticks to separate the seeds from the chaff.

Handstone

Chaff

Seeds

Quern

- Wheat seeds were ground into flour on a quern stone.

Wild and Farmed Food

People in the Neolithic still hunted and caught fish as well as farming. They gathered wild plants to eat such as watercress, nettles, dandelion leaves and wild garlic. For a sweet treat, they collected honey from bees' nests.

Honey

Wild garlic

Everyday Life in the Neolithic

Once people were able to grow food, they could settle in one place and build permanent homes.

Wattle and Daub Houses

At a dig site in Wiltshire, England, archaeologists found evidence of rectangular Neolithic houses made of wattle and daub.

The walls of the house were made by pushing strong hazel rods into the ground. Then more hazel branches were woven through the uprights. This was the wattle. Then the wattle was covered with daub, a ... of chalk, hay and water.

Each house was a single room about 5 metres across. It had a fire in the middle of the room for heating and cooking.

Daub

Wattle

The roof is made of reeds.

A reconstruction of a Neolithic house

A model of Otzi the Iceman ▶

Otzi the Iceman

In 1991, the body of a late Neolithic man was discovered on a mountain range between Italy and Austria. Nicknamed Otzi the Iceman, he was 45 years old and had died about 5300 years ago. After his death, Otzi's body was covered by ice and mummified, or **preserved**.

The fragile remains of Otzi's clothes and shoes gave archaeologists lots of information about Neolithic clothing. Otzi was wearing a bear fur hat and a coat made from strips of goat skin stitched together with **sinew**.

Grow Your Own Clothes

It sounds uncomfortable, but Neolithic people made clothes from stinging nettles! They soaked tough nettle stems in water. Then they carefully stripped soft, silky fibres from the stems. The fibres could be spun and made into yarn for weaving cloth. Flax plants were also grown for the fibres in their stems that were spun and woven into linen.

Flax

A leather belt with a pouch containing tools including a ~~fl~~t knife and scraper.

~~le~~ggings and a loin cloth (underwear) made of goat skin.

Cloth or animal skins were stitched together using needles carved from bone or antler.

Otzi's mummified feet

Deer skin

Brown bear skin

Shoes stuffed with dry grass.

Skara Brae: A Stone Village

In the winter of 1850, a great storm hit the southern shore of Mainland, the biggest of the Orkney Islands, in Scotland.

A Buried Village

The wind and waves tore the grass from a large mound that the islanders called Skerrabra. The storm revealed that under the grass and sandy soil were the remains of a Neolithic village that had been buried for more than 4000 years. Today, the ancient village is known as Skara Brae.

Welcome to Skara Brae

When the village was **excavated**, archaeologists found eight stone houses. The buildings were connected by a series of passageways that allowed the inhabitants to walk from one house to another without going outside.

Stone Age Furniture

Each house was a single room with a doorway that could be closed with a large stone slab. And, because there are hardly any trees in the Orkneys, all the furniture was made of stone!

The passageways were roofed with stone slabs and were just 1 metre high.

The view from a passageway into a house

About 50 to 100 people lived at Skara Brae and it was occupied for about 600 years. Then, around 2200 BC, the village was abandoned and was lost beneath the sand.

Each house had the same stone furniture in the same positions. A stone dresser faced the door. It may have held objects that showed the owner's status and would be the first thing a visitor saw. ▼

The houses were built into grass-covered middens (rubbish heaps). The soil and rubbish helped to keep the houses warm in Orkney's stormy, icy climate.

The roofs of the houses have not survived. They may have been made of driftwood or whale bones covered with turf, animal skins, straw or seaweed.

Box-like stone beds were filled with straw or heather and were covered with sheep or deer skins.

Dresser

Bed

Bed

Fireplace

The villagers probably burned seaweed and animal dung on the fire.

Life At Skara Brae

By studying rubbish in the middens, archaeologists know that the Skara Brae villagers were farmers who grew wheat and barley and raised cattle and sheep. They caught fish such as cod and saithe and collected shellfish to eat and to use as fishing bait. They also ate seabird eggs and hunted deer, wild boar and seals.

The Building of Stonehenge

The people of Neolithic Britain were skilful engineers who built one of the world's most famous ancient monuments — Stonehenge.

The Work Begins

In about 3100 BC, on a wide, open grassland near the modern-day city of Salisbury, people dug a large circular ditch. They dug with tools made from deer antlers. When it was complete, the circular enclosure was 110 metres across, with two entrances into the circle.

The Stones Arrive

About 500 years passed by, and then in 2600 BC, people erected a circle of bluestones within the enclosure. During the next 200 years, they added five trilithons (archway-like structures) and an outer ring all made of enormous sarsen stones. Building Stonehenge required hundreds of workers. But why did Neolithic people build this magnificent structure?

A trilithon

The remains of Stonehenge today

A section of the outer circle

Each sarsen stone weighs about 25 tons and was brought from Marlborough Downs about 32 kilometres from Stonehenge.

The bluestones weigh up to 5 tons each and came from the Preseli Hills in Wales – 250 kilometres from Stonehenge!

How did the builders of ▶ Stonehenge transport the enormous stones over such long distances? Perhaps teams of workers pulled them overland on wooden sledges using tree trunks as rollers (as shown in this reconstruction). They may even have floated them on rafts along rivers.

The upright stones were slid into large holes and then ropes, wooden stakes and people power were used to haul them into an upright position.

The builders used hammerstones of flint and sarsen to shape and smooth the giant stones.

The builders carved tenons (into the upright stones) and mortice holes (into the lintels) so the stones of the outer circle could be tightly fitted together.

Tenons

Mortice holes in a lintel

Hundreds of metres of strong rope had to be made from plant fibres.

Platforms of up to 200 tree trunks were built to lift the lintels onto the uprights.

A Winter Feast at Stonehenge

Today, most experts agree that Stonehenge was a temple, or place of worship and celebration.

Ancient Sunrises and Sunsets

Each year on the morning of the summer **solstice** (midsummer) the Sun rises in line with a pathway through the centre of Stonehenge. On the winter solstice (midwinter), the Sun sets along the same pathway on the opposite side of the circle. The stones were positioned to line up with the movements of the Sun, showing that these times of year were important to ancient people.

At midsummer the Sun rises on this line.

This illustration shows Neolithic people gathering to celebrate the midwinter solstice. ▼

At midwinter the Sun sets on this line.

It's possible that only priests or important members of society were allowed into the centre of the stones.

The Builders' Village

Near to Stonehenge, the remains of a Neolithic settlement have been found. It's been named Durrington Walls and may have contained as many as 1000 houses. Archaeologists think it could be where the Stonehenge builders lived.

A Great Winter Feast

In the middens at Durrington Walls, archaeologists have found 38,000 animal bones, most of which came from pigs. Tests on the pigs' bones and teeth show the animals came from Wales, northern England and even Scotland. Archaeologists could also tell that the pigs were slaughtered in winter. This evidence shows that people came from all over Britain, herding their animals, to enjoy a midwinter feast and celebration at Stonehenge.

Teeth Tell a Story

Like humans, animals grow different kinds of teeth as they get older. Also, an animal's teeth get more worn the older it gets. The teeth found at Durrington Walls belonged to pigs that were about nine months old. The pigs would have been born in spring so if they were nine months old when they died, it proves they were slaughtered in midwinter.

Neolithic pigs probably looked like the animals in this photo.

The winter solstice is the shortest day of the year and falls on the 21st or 22nd of December. After this date, the days start to get longer. Ancient people would have celebrated the fact that spring was on the way and it would soon be time to plant crops.

Stonehenge is in the southwest of England.

21

Neolithic Long Barrows

During the early Neolithic period, people in Britain and Europe built impressive tombs called long barrows.

Stone Tombs

These large mounds of soil can be 100 metres long and 20 metres wide. At one end of the mound there was an entrance. Inside some long barrows the entrance led into a narrow passageway made of stone. Deep inside the mound, small stone chambers, or rooms, led off from the passageway. The remains of the dead were placed inside the chambers.

Ready for the Tomb

Before a body was placed in a long barrow it was usually left outside on a platform in a special place. The body rotted and was eaten by birds and insects until all that was left was the skeleton. This process is called excarnation. The bones were then carefully placed inside the tomb.

The passageway in a long barrow

The Witches Brew

At a Neolithic burial mound in Wales, a mysterious stew-like concoction had been poured onto a fire. Archaeologists discovered that the mixture, nicknamed the "Witches Brew", contained fish, eel, frog, toad, grass snake, mouse, shrew and hare. The stew had been covered with limpet shells and pebbles. Was the mysterious mixture left as a meal for the dead, or was it part of a magical ritual?

A Home for the Dead

Some long barrows contain the remains of up to 50 people, including men, women and children. Archaeologists think it's likely a long barrow was a place where a small community placed all their dead.

Belas Knap Long Barrow

The Belas Knap long barrow has a false main entrance – it doesn't lead anywhere! The chambers in this tomb were reached from the sides of the barrow. It's possible the false entrance was a "spirit door". It would have been built not for the living, but to allow the dead inside to come and go.

Belas Knap long barrow ▼

Side entrance

False main entrance

Burials at Stonehenge

Some people in the Neolithic were cremated and then their remains were buried. At Stonehenge archaeologists have found cremated remains buried inside the stone circle. Possibly these were the burials of important members of society.

The Bronze Age Begins

In about 2400 BC, a new group of people came to Britain from Europe. They brought with them the knowledge of how to make metal.

The Beaker People

Archaeologists call these people the Beaker people after the pottery beakers, or drinking cups, that they made. They came to Britain in boats powered by oarsmen, bringing with them goods for trading, such as farm animals, jewellery, pottery and metal objects.

New Settlers

For many years archaeologists didn't know if the Beaker people stayed in Britain, or if they passed on their metalworking skills to the Britons and then returned home to Europe. Now scientists have discovered that the Beaker people settled in Britain.

▲
Beaker pots were decorated with lines by pressing twisted cord into the clay while it was still soft.

The Start of the Bronze Age

Across the country the knowledge of how to make copper and bronze spread. The Neolithic period in Britain was over and the Bronze Age had begun!

DNA Tells the Story

Scientists tested the DNA of many Bronze Age skeletons in Britain. Some skeletons have the DNA of Neolithic Britons. But most skeletons have Beaker DNA. This evidence shows that in the centuries after the Beaker migration, the Neolithic population of Britain died out. It was replaced by people with Beaker DNA whose **ancestors** had migrated from Europe.

The Amesbury Archer

The Amesbury Archer

In 2002 archaeologists excavated the grave of a Bronze Age man in Amesbury, just a few kilometres from Stonehenge. The man was buried with around 100 objects, which shows he was probably an important member of society. The grave goods included three copper knives, gold earrings and hair ornaments, five beaker pots and four boars' tusks. The grave also held 16 flint arrowheads which have given the man his nickname of the Amesbury Archer.

Tests on the Amesbury Archer show he was aged 35 to 45 when he died. He had spent his childhood in Switzerland, Austria or Germany and was one of the Beaker people.

Bronze Age flint arrowhead

Making Metal

One of the first metals to be shaped and made into objects was copper.

Finding Metal

Early metalworkers chipped rock containing copper from cliffs and hillsides. Using hammerstones, they crushed and ground up the lumps of rock into powder.

Smelting Copper

Next the rocky powder was super-heated over a fire. When the heat reached temperatures of 1100°C, the copper melted and dripped from the rock. This process is known as smelting. The liquid, **molten** copper could then be poured into moulds to make daggers, axe heads and other metal objects.

Rock that contains metal is called ore. Malachite is a type of copper ore.

Molten metal

Bronze Is Invented

In time, metalworkers discovered that if they mixed melted copper and tin, it made a much harder metal — bronze!

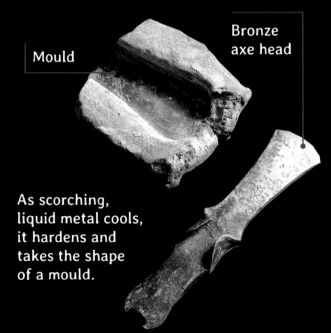

Mould

Bronze axe head

As scorching, liquid metal cools, it hardens and takes the shape of a mould.

Ancient Metal Traders

In Wales, people began to dig deep underground to mine for copper. In Cornwall there were plentiful supplies of tin. People in Britain could now make bronze tools, jewellery and other objects. They could also trade with their European neighbours selling bronze, copper and tin, and objects made from these metals.

An archaeologist in a narrow passageway at the Great Orme copper mine

Finding Tin

In Britain, rock containing tin could be found in the sand and gravel at the bottom of streams in Cornwall. The tin ore had been eroded, or washed away, from hillsides by rain.

Tin ore called cassiterite

The Great Orme Copper Mine

At the Great Orme copper mine in Wales, archaeologists have discovered about 8 kilometres of underground passages. Some of the passages are so narrow, only a child could squeeze into them! During the Bronze Age children went to work down the mines with their parents digging for copper ore with tools made of stone and bone.

Life in the Early Bronze Age

In the early Bronze Age, most people in Britain were still farmers. They lived in small, village-like communities.

Bronze Age Farmers

Axes with strong bronze heads made it easier to cut down trees to clear land for growing crops. Not everyone had metal tools, however. Some people still used stone tools. People also began to divide the land into fields, building low walls of soil and stone.

Enough Food for Everyone

Wheat and barley were the main crops. Farmers also grew chickpeas, lentils, peas, malt for making a beer-like alcoholic drink, and hay and straw for animal feed. If the harvest was good, there was plenty of food for the whole village all year round.

Bronze Age Homes

In the early Bronze Age people built round wattle and daub houses. The roofs were covered with thatch (bunches of straw or reeds) or turf. The roundhouse's door faced the east to catch the light of the rising sun. Often, more than one family shared the house.

Turf roof

A reconstruction of a Bronze Age house

Wattle and daub

Bronze Age Crafts

Bronze Age people no longer had to spend time foraging for wild food. Now they had more time for crafts such as metalworking, pottery and making jewellery and baskets.

A Bronze Age weaving loom

A Cape Made of Gold

Bronze Age craftspeople were highly skilled at making objects from gold.

People obtained gold by digging mines and by searching for nuggets of gold that had eroded from rocks and been washed into streams.

Gold nugget

The Mold Gold Cape was discovered by workers in a burial mound in Mold, Wales, in the 1800s. The cape is so small it could only have fitted the shoulders of a child or a slim woman. It's possible this beautiful cape was once worn by a priestess or maybe a Bronze Age prince or princess.

The cape was skilfully made by hammering and shaping a lump of gold about the size of a table tennis ball.

Wool Clothes

In the Bronze Age, people clipped the wool from sheep using scissor-like, sharp metal shears. The wool was then spun into yarn and woven into cloth for making clothes on a wooden **loom**.

29

Glossary

ancestor
A person from whom you are descended. For example, your great-great-grandparents.

archaeologist
A scientist who studies the past by examining the physical remains left behind, for example buildings, skeletons and tools.

climate
The temperature and weather in an area over a long period of time.

culture
A group of people with a shared way of life. Traditions, celebrations, art and food are all part of a group's culture.

DNA
The material that carries all the information about how a living thing will look and function. DNA is short for deoxyribonucleic acid.

domesticated
Tamed and kept as a pet or farm animal.

evidence
Information that can be used to show that something is true.

excavate
To dig out or remove something from soil or rock.

extinct
Gone forever.

fossilised
Preserved as a rocky fossil.

ice age
A period in time when thick ice sheets covered vast areas of land. Ice ages lasted for millions of years.

loom
A device used for weaving cloth. On a loom, horizontal threads are woven back and forth through vertical threads.

Mesolithic
The middle part of the Stone Age. In Britain this period lasted from about 9500 BC until 4500 BC.

midden
A rubbish dump from history. Archaeologists find objects in middens that tell them about the past.

molten
Turned into a liquid by extreme heating.

Neolithic
The last part of the Stone Age. In Britain this period lasted from about 4500 BC until 2000 BC.

Palaeolithic
The first part of the Stone Age. In Britain this period lasted from about 900,000 years ago until about 9500 BC.

pigment
A substance that can be used to add colour to another material.

prehistory
A time in a people's history before they used a written language. In Britain, prehistory begins about 800,000 years ago and ends when the Romans invaded and began to keep written records.

preserve
To stop something from rotting, or being damaged or destroyed.

scavenge
To feed on the flesh of an animal that's already dead.

sinew
A tough, cord-like length of tissue in a person or animal's body. Tendons and ligaments are both types of sinew.

solstice
The longest and shortest days of the year. In the Northern Hemisphere, the longest day occurs in June (summer solstice) and the shortest day in December (winter solstice).

species
Different types of living things. The members of an animal species look alike and can produce young together.

tomb
A building or other structure where a dead body is laid to rest.